Memories of a
Small-Town Cop

MEMORIES OF A SMALL-TOWN COP

G. DOUGLAS WARD

iUniverse, Inc.
Bloomington

Memories of a Small-Town Cop

iUniverse books may be ordered through booksellers or by contacting:

iUniverse
1663 Liberty Drive
Bloomington, IN 47403
www.iuniverse.com
1-800-Authors (1-800-288-4677)

ISBN: 978-1-4620-7348-1 (sc)
ISBN: 978-1-4620-7350-4 (hc)
ISBN: 978-1-4620-7349-8 (ebk)

Printed in the United States of America

iUniverse rev. date: 12/22/2011

On any night you can watch police programs which show officers fighting crime using high tech equipment. But what did officers use before onboard computers and other high tech gear? Try common sense, guts and a lot of luck.

Well buckle up and hang on as I take you on a ten year journey that will make you laugh, make you cry and even make you wonder why. This is the journey of a small town cop.

CONTENTS

- Dedication ix
- About the Author...xi
- Planting the Seeds 1
- Could have been my dad 3
- Ham sandwich anyone 4
- Always keep a sheet of plastic in the trunk...............................6
- Caught by an old rotary phone 7
- Case of the missing body..8
- Putting on the badge...10
- Basic Training 12
- You make the decision 13
- On the Job Training 14
- I don't want to see somebody naked 15
- Temper, Temper..16
- Only having on your socks is just wrong 17
- It's the uniform 18
- What the heck is a Mojo?...19
- Another Mojo Moment 20
- Can you be a cop and a friend too?... 21
- Doing the right thing is always good..22
- It's a bird, it's a plane, it's...23
- Don't do as I do . . . do as I say. 25
- It's not what you say it's how you say it................................... 26
- Sometimes you just have to say something or bust 27
- A few minutes can make a big difference 28
- Small town speed trap 29
- I think I'll kill my wife today.. 30
- There's No Place like Home!... 31
- Grabbed from the Grave 32
- River Dance! 33
- The Western gunfight.. 34
- Having children makes a difference...35
- Some people just don't learn 38
- 140 MPH, what was I thinking? 39
- Ever had one of those days?.. 40
- Never mess with old timers 42
- Driving under the influence of love 44

- Same thing, different night!.. 45
- For heaven's sake, get a room 46
- "I would like to respectfully refuse to testify" 47
- Twelve ticked off lawmen 49
- Quick response time.. 50
- Repeat event on a different night 51
- Drunk drivers do crazy things 52
- A scary night on the East side 54
- Don't tell me Gut Feelings don't work.. 56
- The continued attraction of vending machines 59
- Never drink when committing a crime 60
- Dress for Success before you break in...61
- Don't be thankful for a quiet night until it's over 63
- Call it what it is, a homicide 65
- Sometimes there is no justice 66
- Dead bodies ruin your day...68
- No ma'am, you're not dying on my shift 70
- Playing tricks on fellow officers helped brighten spirits 71
- The best trick ever on a fellow officer..72
- Being a breathalyzer operator..73
- One breathalyzer test that scared me 74
- A college education may be overrated!...75
- Ever been hit by the President of the United States?...................77
- Always keep one eye on the Sergeant 79
- How do old Sergeants stay safe so long? 80
- Threatening an officer's family is NOT a good idea! 81
- Putting life in perspective 83
- A Great Doctor 84
- Not much sympathy for hardheaded people................................. 85
- Lady, you weren't speeding . . . you were flying low................... 86
- Every town has a Charlie Boy 87
- Then there was Buddy..89
- Don't tick off my partner!... 90
- Monnie got me this time 91
- Big Monkey 92
- The Big squeeze.. 94
- Losing a best friend 95
- Time to try something else.. 96
- Good things come to those who wait. 97
- A Highway Patrol Story 98
- A Stand-in Mother Duck 99
- Change is good 101
- Memories of a Small Town Cop...103

DEDICATION

This book is dedicated to my wife and all the spouses of police officers, firemen and rescue personnel everywhere. Being a police officer was not easy but being the spouse of an officer was and is more difficult than you could ever imagine. Many nights while working third shift I would drive by my home to see my wife looking from our bedroom window trying to catch a glimpse of me. I would pull up beside her bedroom window, cut the car off and we would talk a few minutes until she felt she could finally go to sleep. She knew from stories I told her roughly when the most dangerous issues took place around our small peaceful town. Even though I would tell her not to worry she always would. She never complained because she knew I loved my job.

Thanks for loving me without question for 42 years. You are, have always been and will always be my best friend.

A Little about the Author

My family moved to Tarboro, North Carolina in 1952 when the population was around ninety five hundred residents. Today, the population is still around ninety five hundred people. Our town billboard always read, "Tarboro, A Town Geared for Progress!" Unfortunately our small town never got out of first gear.

My law enforcement career began in April of 1972. After being sworn in I had the opportunity to see just how crazy, how mean, how peculiar and how funny people could be.

Serious crimes didn't take place in our small town, or so I thought. As a police officer and a breathalyzer operator I was about to find out just how quiet my town really was.

My ten law enforcement years were filled with never ending experiences. I worked hard at my job because I loved it so much. The townspeople recognized that too and presented me with the "Officer of the Year" award in 1976. I was extremely proud to be recognized by the citizens for whom I worked. Today I still display this award proudly.

My mindset in and out of law enforcement has always been to protect myself at all times and go home safely at the end of my shift. That is still my goal today.

PLANTING THE SEEDS

My father was a deputy sheriff in the 60's in our fairly large county. The sheriff's department had only five deputies, a chief deputy and a sheriff to cover the large area twenty four hours a day. During his first couple of years as a deputy there were no law enforcement vehicles. The deputies had to use their own personal cars. The emergency lights were red and had to be placed on the dash board and plugged into the cigarette lighter. His siren was the old air type and not the electronic "yelpers" used today. The family car sure got a daily workout. His first real departmental patrol car was issued to him in 1969. Receiving a new high performance Ford with a 429 cubic inch police interceptor engine was like an early Christmas for the deputies.

I believe my dad's law enforcement experiences planted the seeds for me one day becoming a law enforcement officer. Allow me to share with you some of his experiences so you can understand from where my interest came.

One evening during my early high school years my dad's car radio P.A. system sounded off reporting an accident three miles from our home. The rescue squad had already passed our home at a high rate of speed responding to the accident. Dad looked at me and said, *"Want to go to a wreck?"* This was the first time he had ever asked me to go with him on a call. My heart went into overdrive as I blurted out *"YES!"* We both jumped in his patrol car and away we went. Two minutes later we were pulling up to the accident scene. The accident was caused when a car, traveling out of town at a high rate of speed, reached a sharp left curve in the road and failed to negotiate the turn. The vehicle kept straight across a residential yard and into a very large pine tree. The pine tree was so big it didn't budge when struck. The impact threw the occupants out of their vehicle. I noticed one of the men under the tree on his back looking up so I walked up to him and asked him if he was OK. Dad walked up to me and whispered,

"He won't be answering son . . . he's dead!" I stood there a few moments staring at the man not believing what I was seeing. He was really dead! I walked away with a strange feeling sorrow for him and his family. This would not be my last experience with the death of human beings but it was my first time seeing a traffic fatality. I was surprised how calm I was having seen this for the first time.

COULD HAVE BEEN MY DAD

Late one night, I was sitting at home watching TV when dad came through the back door very upset. His crying was uncontrollable and this was something I had never seen from my dad. That night after mom had put him to bed, she came back into the kitchen to tell me what had happened.

Dad had received a call to respond to a drunk and disorderly person on the opposite side of the county. His co-worker called him on the radio and said he was a little closer and would take the call if dad would back him up. My dad told him he was on the way. When the deputy arrived at the little country store he stepped out of his patrol vehicle and asked what the problem was. The people standing around pointed at a man who stood on the opposite side of the deputy's patrol vehicle. As the deputy turned to talk to the man the suspect raised a double barrel shotgun over the hood of the deputy's car and fired both barrels into the deputy's face and upper head. My dad and another deputy arrived minutes later and called for rescue. The shooter had staggered down the railroad tracks and into a residence trying to hide from the law. He was found and taken into custody. The deputy had already been rushed to the hospital where he passed away a few hours later. That call was supposed to have been my dad's call. The deputy killed that night was a handsome young man with a wife and small child. The murderer, due to politics and a slick lawyer, only stayed in prison a short time and was released from prison. The murderer's habits today are the same as they were back then, drinking until intoxicated and passing out wherever he happens to fall. The difference is he is alive and a fine officer, husband and father is not. I often wonder what would have happened if my dad had been first to arrive. Isn't it funny how our laws go to great lengths to protect criminals but never the victims?

Ham Sandwich Anyone

Another incident happened when my dad and the chief deputy responded to an apartment out in a nice quiet wooded area of the county. The renter had come home earlier with groceries to find someone had broken in and believed the person was still in the house. The chief deputy went to the front door while my dad and the landlord entered the back door and into the kitchen. Dad was carrying his standard .38 caliber hand gun and had given the landlord a department issued sawed off double barreled shotgun loaded with buckshot. What happened next is scary to think about even today. The intruder was still inside and had taken a Civil War saber from above the fireplace mantle. He had it in his hands when dad entered through the back kitchen door. The landlord has split off from dad walking into the living room. The burglar, hearing the entry, walked into the kitchen, spotted my dad and headed straight for him with saber in hand. Dad yelled for him to drop the sword but the attacker kept advancing. He drew back the sword and, like Babe Ruth trying to hit a home run, swung for dad's head. Dad fired twice with his .38 Special striking the man in the shoulder and the lower abdomen. The second shot brought the man down. The sword passed three inches above dad's head and buried itself about three inches into the solid wood door. The shots being fired scared the landlord so much he pulled both triggers on the shotgun removing one of the armrests on the living room couch. As it turned out the attacker had escaped from a mental hospital and, after being on the run, was looking for something to eat. Dad must have looked like a ham sandwich to him.

Respect for Law Week with my dad, wife and son

Always keep a sheet of plastic in the trunk

I asked my dad, now 89, to tell me a funny story from his days as a deputy. The request had barely left my lips when he started laughing. He said he and the chief deputy received a call one night about a body having been seen lying beside a road near railroad tracks near the town of Mildred six miles out of Tarboro. When they arrived they found a man dead . . . dead drunk! The man was well known by law enforcement personnel for his consumption of alcohol. To make things worse he had defecated on himself. Because the sheriff's department, at that time, had to use their own personal vehicle as a patrol car the chief deputy knew he couldn't leave the man there and he was not going to put the smelling individual in his back seat. So he opened the drunk of his car, opened a plastic sheet onto which he and my dad placed the drunken man. The chief deputy closed the trunk and transported him to the county jail radioing ahead so prison trustees could meet them outside to remove the man from the trunk. Upon arriving the trustees removed the individual from the trunk of the car and took him down to the prison showers.

When you are forced to use your own vehicle it pays to be prepared.

Caught by an Old Rotary Phone

You more mature lawmen will enjoy this story because it involves an old trick used to catch people who before this night kept getting away with breaking in, taking money and causing a lot of damage. The American Legion building held numerous vending machines and over a four month period was broken into numerous times with no particular pattern being set. Keep in mind this happened before touchtone phones when everyone had to use rotary dial phones.

I was up late on a Saturday night watching Shock Theatre on TV and dad had already come home for the night and was in bed. At about 1:00 A.M. the phone rang and I answered it. I said hello twice but no one answered. Then I heard dad's feet hit the floor. He took the phone from my hands and listened for a few seconds. He then hung the phone up and slipped into his uniform like the house was on fire. He ran out the door of the house, jumped into his patrol car and was gone like the wind. The next morning I found out what had happened.

Anyone familiar with the old rotary phones knows where the finger stop was located on the dial. What dad had done was set a phone string trap at the American Legion. He tied a piece of string to the top of the American Legion office door, ran the string up and over the room to a phone located on office desk. The other end of the string was attached to a short piece of pencil. Dad had dialed our home number and when he dialed the last digit he lodged the pencil in at the finger stop in the phone dial. When these young hoods broke into the building this time, they pulled open the door and the string pulled the pencil out of the phone dial which completed the phone call circuit which called our house. This trick worked without a hitch and dad got there in time to catch the thieves who were still inside the building. The old investigative ways were remarkable compared to today's standards.

CASE OF THE MISSING BODY

A neighboring county called for assistance with an investigation they believed to be a murder. A river that runs just outside this small town was experiencing low water level due to the lack of rain in the area but the fishing in that river was still excellent. The low water level revealed rocks and debris in the river which was not really an issue. But this time it revealed something which almost scared one would be fisherman to death. What he saw in the rocks near the river bank was a pair of human legs. When he made the discovery the fisherman immediately notified the local police. The legs found however were not attached to a body. They had been severed just below the knees. Authorities firmly believed there had been a murder and dismemberment so they began a search up and down the river in an effort to find the rest of the body. The search proved unsuccessful. Upon checking the nearby town for missing person reports or any unusual activity the mystery deepened. No one in this little town was reported missing.

As it turned out a nearby funeral home had to supply a casket for a recently deceased man. The family couldn't afford to buy a new casket for their family member nor did the funeral home have a casket to fit him so the two entities agreed to make the deceased fit into the smaller casket they had in stock and one the family could afford. The funeral home removed the deceased person's legs and threw them in the river believing the legs would float away never to be seen again. Once the truth came out no charges were made in this case. True story . . . I swear!

After many years as a deputy, dad was appointed Chief Magistrate for the county. A job he would keep for almost 30 years. Being a deputy before becoming a Magistrate helped him greatly in his new position.

PUTTING ON THE BADGE

At the age of 21, I was sworn in as a police officer by my father, the chief magistrate of the county. This took place in April of 1972 and I still remember the words he said as he finished the swearing in process. He ended with "Congratulations you are now a first class S.O.B. and going with every woman in town." I stared at him and he smiled at me saying, "Get used to it. You're going to be accused of it whether you like it or not. It comes with wearing a badge." Later on, I would understand what he meant.

BASIC TRAINING

Basic training for a police officer back in 1972 only lasted about 4 weeks. There was no physical training involved or trips to a firing range, only a basic teaching of federal and state laws. Different scenarios were given and we had to discuss them and decide what we could and could not do as law enforcement officers. Here is one of the true story scenarios given to us.

You make the decision

A man is driving a tanker filled with fuel oil when his rig is forced off the road and overturns. Due to non existent seat-belt laws the driver is thrown from his rig and his legs are pinned under the tanker which is leaking fuel oil. A trooper arrives on the scene with rescue and fire personnel still twenty minutes away. The victim, still conscious but in pain, sees fuel oil is leaking and his truck has now caught fire with fuel oil creeping toward him bringing fire with it. The truck driver cannot get his legs free and knows rescue will not get there in time. He realizes what kind of death he is about to experience and wants no part of burning alive. He asked then begged the trooper to shoot him pleading, "I don't want to die this way and burn to death!" The trooper tells him he can't do that. The man then begs for the trooper to give him his revolver so he can take his own life before the fire reaches him. Now comes the question we were asked. What would you do? I can't tell you the answer . . . you have to decide. Just imagine being the trooper having to make that decision and having to hear the pleas of a man who is about to die. What would you have done had you been the trooper?

On the Job Training

Then came the time I had to be paired up with a training officer whose job was to prepare me for the time when I would work by myself. The person who trained me was nice guy and good trainer but he also had a temper. Luckily his temper showed itself very little during training.

I DON'T WANT TO SEE SOMEBODY NAKED

One of his quirks was to check couples who were parking to see if he could catch them naked. He would patrol the lover's lanes with his lights out until he saw a parked car with windows that were fogged up. He would then pull up to within twenty feet or so, walk up quickly with his flashlight and shine it in the window. More often than not he would catch them in a compromising position. Of course he would keep the light mostly on the female and advise them they would need to move on due to criminal activity in the area. They would quickly get their clothes on and leave the area. He would then come back to the car and give a detailed description of what he had seen while laughing. One night he saw a vehicle with fogged up car windows. He said, "Listen, when I pull up beside the car you jump out and shine your light inside." Without hesitation I told him I would not. He looked at me and asked (angrily) why not. I told him that if I did and the man in the vehicle got out and kicked my ass I couldn't blame him. Well, my training officer called me chicken sh*t and drove on. It didn't bother me because I knew I had made the right decision. He didn't ask me again either.

Temper, Temper

There was another time we I stopped a drunk driver around two in the morning. The man was obviously under the influence of alcohol and was placed under arrest. After he cuffed the suspect he searched the driver's left pants pocket while I searched his right side. Well wouldn't you know it that while the officer had his hands in the man's left front pocket the intoxicated driver looked straight at him and slurred the words, "I know what you're trying to do . . . you're trying to feel of my peter!" This struck me as funny and I started laughing. Then I noticed my training officer who obviously didn't find the suspect's words funny. He became angry, grabbed the man's belt and snatched the intoxicated man forward causing him to fall forward onto the rocky pavement. Did I mention that this man was very tall and heavy? When he started to fall he was so big there was no way in hell we could stop the fall. When his head hit the pavement it sounded like a ripe watermelon. The angry officer was no longer angry . . . he was scared. I looked at my trainer and asked him why he had done such a thing. We had to transport him to the hospital which is routine when blood was involved. Luckily, he only needed cleaning up and a couple of Band Aids. I lost a lot of respect for my training officer that night. Fortunately the man was so intoxicated that night he didn't remember anything. I reported the incident to the Sergeant after the training officer reported that the suspect lost his balance and fell. This officer later left our department and went to another department some thirty miles away. Wrong is wrong. Fortunately these types of incidents are rare. The vast majority of officers are very ethical making every effort to do the right thing on a regular basis.

ONLY HAVING ON YOUR SOCKS IS JUST WRONG

One of the older sergeants was called to the East side of town to back up the ABC (Alcohol Beverage Control) department. They were about to serve a search warrant on a house known for bootleg liquor, marijuana and prostitution. The search warrant was for illegal liquor and the ABC department wanted the sergeant to enter through the back door when they went through the front door. This placed the sergeant entering the kitchen area where he searched for contraband and finding none. He then opened a kitchen door known as a food closet and there in front of him stood a very well known upper class business man wearing nothing but a pair of socks and a scared look. The Sergeant looked up and down the naked business owner and said, "Well, Hell . . . Everybody's got to be somewhere don't they?" He then allowed the man to slip out the back door and into the darkness. When the ABC men made their way to the kitchen the Sergeant told them he found nothing in that area. The Sergeant would not tell me who the man was but he did say that up until the day the business man died, if he would see the Sergeant on the street he would cross to the other side of the street and turn his head due to still being embarrassed.

It's the uniform

Apparently there are some girls and women who have an attraction for any man in a uniform. This causes distractions especially when they follow the patrol vehicle around while the officer is patrolling the beat. There was a pretty young blonde lady who would spot me when I worked second or third shift. On one particular Saturday night she was riding around my beat and she started following my patrol vehicle. It just so happened I had a reserve officer with me who was recently divorced. I started a conversation with him about dating and asked if he would be interested in meeting a young lady. "Sure" was the reply so I pulled up beside the young lady and let them speak to each other. He left me early that night and she picked him up at the police station. When I saw him again I asked him how his date went. He said she took him straight over to lover's lane. He had a big smile on his face telling me they had enjoyed themselves greatly that night. I asked if he got her name. He said no. He did say after they hooked up she asked him his name. He answered her by giving her my name. My first thought was I hope she doesn't call my house. Dad's swearing in words came to mind when this episode happened.

WHAT THE HECK IS A MOJO?

When I was first released to be on my own I had the downtown beat and that means I was on foot in a six block business area until most of the businesses closed around five PM. The characters downtown normally would hang around two particular corners where wine and beer was sold and they knew a rookie cop when they saw one. Seems like each time I passed those two corners on foot someone would say something derogatory while mingling in small groups. Son-of-a-b**ch and M-F seemed to be the favorite words spoken but I could never tell who was making the comments. When I told my working buddy about the language and the staring when I passed by he said "Try wearing a Mojo." Of course I had never heard the word so he told me some people, many of whom stood around those two street corners, were very superstitious and they were scared of a Mojo. Asking a second time what a Mojo is he told me to get a clear medicine container and put odd objects inside until it looks very weird. I figured what the hell so I got the container and in it I placed a small marble, a bird feather, a couple of drops of food coloring, a little oil and water, sand and a couple of other things I actually don't remember. I placed a small chain through the top making sure it was sealed and attached it to my belt on the side that would be exposed and near my revolver to make sure it would be seen. I remember it was on a Friday and the streets were full of great folks especially around those two corners. I remember walking past the corners the first time and being on the receiving end of the normal verbal abuse. But a strange thing happened. A great deal of whispering took place as I walked away from the group heading down the sidewalk. The next time I passed the two corners there wasn't a soul in sight. Seriously, not one person! That was one of the first truly strange experiences I had experienced alone. Realizing how superstitious people were would come into play many times in my law enforcement career.

Another Mojo Moment

I had a first cousin who decided to try his hand in the Probation and Parole area of law enforcement. He was two counties over from mine but the people there were just as strange about their beliefs as the people in my area. He had a probationer who was not keeping his court ordered appointments so he went to the probationer's residence. He knocked on the door numerous times and could hear the TV playing inside and even heard it turn off but no one would answer the door. He yelled into the door, "That's OK, I've got something for you!" He then walked to his car, backed out of the driveway, parked the vehicle, opened his trunk and took out a plain bag. He then walked along the driveway and front yard of the residence speaking a language no one could identify while sprinkling white powder on the ground as he walked. He placed the bag back in the car and started driving away. As he pulled away he looked back at the house and saw at least three sets of eyes looking out at him from the curtains and blinds. By the time he got back to his office there were eleven phone messages from the family of the probationer's relatives pleading with him to come get the man and remove the curse he had placed on the family.

Now that's funny right there, I don't care who you are that's funny right there!

CAN YOU BE A COP AND A FRIEND TOO?

A gentleman who worked with the phone company was coming into town one day when he entered a 35 mph zone where I was working radar. His speed was well in excess of the posted speed so the radar locked on and I stopped him and issued a citation. Until the last time I saw him he would always bring up that citation and not in a nice way. Even at a ceremony honoring my dad for his long service in a certain civic organization he managed to bring up that citation in front of the crowd and express his displeasure and this is thirty five years later. Through the years he never denied speeding. He just felt like he should have been given a break. In reality real friends wouldn't expect a break. Real friends would expect you to do your job.

Did I give breaks? Sure I did but not in a wholesale way. If I felt someone deserved a break I would cut them a little break. It didn't matter about gender, race or age. Respect begot respect. Since leaving Police work I have met many people I had arrested in the past. One of those people approached me in a store one day and said, "You don't remember me, do you?" I replied I did not. He said, "You arrested me for drunk driving a few years ago." I told him he looked familiar but I still didn't remember the arrest. He then said the words all officers like to hear. He said, "You know what . . . it's the best damned thing that ever happened to me!" "I haven't had anything to drink since you caught me so it turned out to be a good thing." He then extended his hand, which I took and smiled saying, "It's nice to see you again." Now there was a friend I didn't know I had.

DOING THE RIGHT THING IS ALWAYS GOOD

Late one morning, while working first shift, I set up my radar unit to work a 35 mph zone on the North end of our Main Street. As was routine before working any speed zone I would ride that zone to verify the speed limit. That's exactly what I did on this morning before calibrating my radar and starting operation. It wasn't long before I issued my first citation, then my second, third and fourth. The fourth driver was adamant in his belief the zone he was in was 45 mph and not a 35. Because it was very unusual to have so many citations in such a short period of time and to be on the safe side I drove through the speed zone again. Wouldn't you just know it? While I was working radar in my speed zone the State of North Carolina was around the curve changing all of the 35 mph speed limit signs to 45 mph. Having a copy of all the citations written at that location I stopped what I was doing and traveled to the police to tell the police chief what had happened. He made sure the people who received citations were notified not to appear in court and explained the citations would be voided.

It's a Bird, It's a Plane, It's

Our department was very small numbering about twenty six people. Our normal patrol numbers excluding reserve officers was three people per shift. One covering the North end of town, one on the South end of town and a sergeant covering the East and West side of a town of ninety five hundred people was the norm. One third shift night I was dispatched to the mayor's home for reasons unknown. As I pulled up in front of the home the mayor's family was in the front yard which was unusual due to the time of night which was early morning after one A.M. I asked the family what the problem was and they all pointed toward the Northeast sky where a light could be seen hovering above a tall oak tree about five hundred yards away. This light was not landing lights, not a helicopter and not a balloon. It also kept changing colors. We all stood there and watched it for a couple of minutes as the object remained motionless. The sergeant on duty pulled up and asked me what was going on. I showed him the curious lights. He called the dispatcher and requested Seymour Johnson Air Force Base (sixty miles to our South) send a jet to our location to identify this phenomenon. Less than fifteen minutes later we heard and saw two F4 Phantoms screaming across the sky heading left to right directly toward the light. As the two Phantoms closed in on the light it started to move and move it did. Although Seymour Johnson officially said their pilots saw nothing they were obviously in hot pursuit of the object until out of our sight. When I left the mayor's house I rode by my own residence three blocks away where my wife was watching out of the bedroom window. She waved me over and asked, "Did you see those strange lights above that tree?" Like I said in the dedication, she didn't sleep well when I worked third shift. I told her what had just happened and she was as excited as a child seeing Santa for the first time.

Don't do as I do . . . do as I say.

Early one afternoon a call came into the station reporting a man had just assaulted a female with a knife and was walking Northwest on the loop road. The sergeant on duty picked up a rookie and went looking for the man. They soon found him on foot walking out of town approaching the city limits. The sergeant dropped off the rookie about twenty five yards behind the suspect while the Sergeant pulled the patrol car about twenty five yards in front of the knife toting man. The suspect quickly realized that he had an officer in front of him and one behind him. Due to his criminal record he quickly sized up the situation and turned toward the officer he could identify as a rookie and started walking toward him with knife drawn. The rookie took out his revolver and aimed at the suspect. The sergeant shouted to the rookie to put away his gun and get out his night stick. The sergeant had to tell him twice because the rookie couldn't believe what he was hearing. Following his instructions the rookie holstered his revolver and pulled out his night stick. Then without warning the suspect turned around and headed straight toward the sergeant who immediately pulled out his revolver and fired two rounds striking the suspect in the upper chest and stomach. Rescue arrived and took the suspect to the hospital where he recovered and later charged. When the two officers returned to the station and began to talk of the incident the rookie had to ask the one question that was worrying the living crap out of him. "Sergeant, why did you tell me to put away my gun and pull out my night stick then you pulled your gun and shot him twice?" The sergeant without hesitation replied, "Hell, he was coming at me then!"

It's Not What You Say It's How You Say It

During my first year as an officer it was popular to refer to the Police as pigs if you were in your early teens or just wanted to show disrespect. The name calling never set very well with me. Anyway, one afternoon I was patrolling the North end of town beside the Ford dealership. As I passed by with my window down several young children started making oink-oink noises and finally one or two of the kids yelled out "PIG!" I slammed on brakes and turned into the used car side of the dealership and was able to see these kids as they ducked down behind several cars in an attempt to hide from me. I cut my patrol car off, walked to the middle of the lot and called for them to come out which they did. When I looked at them my anger quickly faded due to their ages and the look of fear on their faces. I took a deep breath and said, "I'm not going to ask you who you are, who made the oink noises or called out pig because it doesn't really matter. What does matter is that you understand this ... if you ever need my help, if your brother or sister ever needs my help, if you Mom or Dad ever needs my help, I will be there for you!" "If someone tries to hurt you, break into your home or steal your property, I will be there for you!" "And I will be there no matter what names you call me because that's my job and I want you safe!" "Now go home and think about what you did today." All the kids walked off with their heads down without a word being said. About an hour later at shift change I walked into the station and the desk sergeant asked, "Did you have a talk with some kids at the Ford place this afternoon?" Just knowing I was in trouble because you never know what the kid's version to their parents would be, I quickly answered "No" and kept walking. The sergeant then said, "Well if you did, I'll tell you one thing, you sure made an impression on those kids and their parents. The parents sure appreciated the way it was handled." Then my memory miraculously recovered and I told the sergeant it was me. But I think he already knew that. Don't you?

SOMETIMES YOU JUST HAVE TO SAY SOMETHING OR BUST

An intersection was assigned to me one day to help a funeral procession pass through unobstructed. A school bus was at the intersection awaiting the end of what seemed like the never ending line of cars. As the hearse passed the school bus quite a few children hung out of the windows jeering and making comments. This bothered me to no end and before the last car passed I had made up my mind what I was going to do even if it got me in trouble. I made sure traffic was back in sync with the traffic lights and returned to my patrol vehicle. When the school bus passed me I pulled in behind it and turned on my blue light. The bus pulled over and I walked up to the bus door which was opened by the driver. I looked at her and said, "This will only take a minute." All the pre-teen occupants were quiet as I walked down the bus aisle. The words just seemed to flow when I spoke these words: "Each one of you should be ashamed of yourself for what you just did. Not only did you show disrespect for a person who just passed away, you missed out on having one of the best and kindest teachers this city has ever known. I'm sorry you will never have the chance to meet her and love her like thousands of kids before you." As I turned around to leave the bus you could have heard a pin drop. The lady driver of the bus spoke to me as I was leaving the bus saying, "Thank you so much for doing that." I turned, winked and nodded at her and felt very good about myself.

A FEW MINUTES CAN MAKE A BIG DIFFERENCE

One quiet Sunday afternoon I was riding with the sergeant on Duty when a call came in from a concerned mother who reported her young son missing. We arrived at her home on in only a couple of minutes. After a brief talk with her and obtaining a description of her five year old son we started walking the area around her home. We were about to put out the description of her son when we both noticed an old refrigerator in the back yard. We both looked at each other and thought the same thing at the same time. I said, "You don't think . . .?" The sergeant replied, "Let's check it to be sure." I opened the refrigerator door and there lying in the bottom of the refrigerator was her son. He opened his eyes, looked up, saw us, climbed out and ran to his Mom. Both the sergeant and I breathed a collective sigh of relief while shaking at the thought of how we would have found him if we had been ten minutes later. The sergeant being the man he was went to the door and gave the Mother hell about leaving a refrigerator in the yard without removing the door. As I recall he was upset for the rest of the shift.

SMALL TOWN SPEED TRAP

I was working radar one day in a thirty five mph zone when a big Fleetwood Cadillac came barreling through my zone at a speed of around sixty mph. Because reciprocal agreements were not being recognized at that time between states, this Washington DC driver had to follow me to the Magistrates office to either post bond or plead guilty and pay a fine. He wasn't happy about it but I had his license and registration in my hand. His unhappiness was increased when we walked into the Magistrates office and I said "Hey Pop" and my dad (the magistrate) replied "Hi, Son." The man looked at me then my dad and said . . . "You have got to be kidding me! I've heard of places like this but . . ." After the man plead guilty, paid his fine and left the office my dad and I just looked at each other and smiled. This was one of many unforgettable Father-Son moments.

I THINK I'LL KILL MY WIFE TODAY

It was on a Friday afternoon when a man decided to pull a handgun and put it to the head of his wife in the parking lot of one of our banks. The officer patrolling the South end of town (on foot) called for back up and I responded with blue light and siren. I wasn't receiving much information on my radio until I pulled into the parking lot of the bank. This was the first time I heard my fellow officer say, "Watch out, he's got a gun!" When I heard the key word gun I slammed on brakes and came to a stop at a location which happened to have a bird's eye view of the man holding a handgun under his wife's neck after throwing her down to the pavement between two parked vehicles. I knew the woman because she worked at the A&P Food Store with my wife. I could tell she was bleeding but I didn't know from what or from where. I knew this, I had to do something. I backed my vehicle up about twenty feet and bailed out quickly working my way behind the man. He never saw me as I reach an area within eight feet of him with gun in hand. I shouted to him to drop his gun and for the first time in my life I was ready to take a life if needed. As he followed my directions and put his revolver down his wife ran to the other officer while I pinned him to the back of a vehicle and cuffed him. To this day the woman refers to me as the man who saved her life. It still feels good to hear it said even thirty five years later. The only thing which bothered us was she refused to file charges against her husband. That was fine with us, she didn't have to . . . we did.

There's No Place like Home!

One of our regular visitors to the police department lobby was a young man who would come to complain to us about us once a week. He would comment about our department being racist, calling us small town honkies, etc. Then came the day when he visited one last time to tell us he was leaving and moving to New York where he didn't have to put up with small town racist cops anymore. He had few words other than those. He then left the lobby and the state. A few months later I entered the lobby at shift change and there stood our friend. We couldn't help ourselves when we asked him why he was back at a place he hated so much and thought was so racist. He said, "Man you guys are all right by me. You guys are nice and I ain't never going to leave here no more." "Man, I was up on a street corner up there in New York when a cop working an intersection told me to cross the street. I told him I would cross when I was G** D*** good and ready. You know that cop came over to me, took out his night stick and beat the sh** out of me! I want you to know I crossed that damn street and then I brought my ass back home." "You guys are all right with me." "Ya'll never treated me that way."

I guess the grass is not always greener on the other side.

Grabbed from the Grave

I have to set this up for you so you can understand how serious this was and what happened to make it so funny so quickly. We were having an issue with a man breaking into homes at night occupied only by single females. He would always enter the home without making any noise, throw the covers up over the faces of the victim so they couldn't identify him, warn them about making any noise then rape them. He would then leave as quietly as he entered. When the women felt he had gone they would call the police.

Now, having said that I will share with you what happened one particular night while we were staked out trying to catch this low life criminal. Two officers were in unmarked dark cars, I was on a roof top in the cover of tree limbs and my working partner, Monnie, was in a church cemetery behind a four foot brick wall. The cemetery was so dark you could see out of it toward the street lights but no one could see into the resting place of the dead. Beside the brick wall was the sidewalk.

Well it just so happened on this night a person with a long criminal record for drinking and being disorderly happened to be walking past that cemetery wall. He was acting very nervous and would not look into the cemetery where my partner was staked out behind the wall. We knew this man was a drunk and a thief but also knew he didn't have the intestinal fortitude for rape or burglary. Anyway, when this guy walked to the spot where Monnie was behind the brick wall Monnie raised up from behind the cemetery wall, reached over the wall, grabbed him on the shoulder and yelled, "WHAT YOU DOING?" The man never looked to see who or what grabbed his shoulder. He just hit a gear we didn't know he had and the last time we saw him he was still in high gear running across the river bridge (city limits) showing no signs of slowing down. We didn't see him for days after that.

We never caught our rapist but we did receive information he was from up North and stopped visiting our little town.

River Dance!

Our department had an outstanding theft warrant for the (cemetery) man in the previous story. He was spotted coming across the river bridge heading into our town so one of our community service men waited on our side of the bridge while the other town's police chief approached him from the other side. The suspect saw that he was trapped between law enforcement agencies so he climbed over the side of the bridge and stood on a water pipe while shouting "Come any closer and I'll jump!" Of course our man yelled back at him to "Go ahead . . . JUMP!" Never figured he would. He did! One of our marked cars drove down to the River Road and found the suspect. No he wasn't dead. He wasn't even hurt because the river table was low and he managed to land in a large area of mud in which he was stuck up to his waist. We got our muddy man and put him in our clean jail.

THE WESTERN GUNFIGHT

Our neighboring police chief was not only the head law enforcement officer in his small town he was also the town's electrician. It was not unusual to see him up a utility pole wearing short pants, long sleeve camouflage shirt, boots, his revolver and a hard hat while working on a power line. He was quite a character, but we could always count on him to back us up if called upon.

A few years, before I became an officer, this police chief and one of his officers were playing a card game at one of his town's hangouts when they got into a serious argument. So angry were the two men that they agreed to do the Old West thing and have a gunfight and may be best (fastest) man win. The two men faced off and drew their weapons. The chief's shot proved deadly and the ensuing trial found him innocent after he plead self defense.

Having Children Makes a Difference

During my second year as an officer my wife gave birth to our first child, a son born to us on October 11th 1973. On December 24th 1973 the following incident happened which made me appreciate how important family was.

A call came in to the station from a prominent attorney saying the Police were needed at a particular address on Saint Patrick Street in the historic district but there was no further information. My working partner, Monnie, arrived first and was behind a big tree looking toward a two story home with his gun drawn. I arrived and stepped out of my car and asked him what was going on. He said, "Watch yourself, he's got a gun!" (Sound familiar?) I ducked down and ran to a location behind a vehicle parked in front of the home which was about forty feet from the door. Lying in the doorway, which was open, was a man with a known history of drug problems. He was in his briefs lying on his stomach pointing a twelve gauge shotgun out of the front door. Twelve inches of the gun barrel was exposed from the doorway and pointing in Monnie's direction. Knowing we had to do something I was able to work my way around to the far end of the porch where his wife stood with the attorney who had called in the complaint. Having known her for years I asked her if the gun was loaded. "Gerald, I really don't know" was her answer. I then made up my mind what I was going to do. I slipped off my shoes, belt, gun and anything else (patent leather and noisy) which would give me away and crawled up on the porch. I looked over at Monnie who is an excellent shot in case I missed my opportunity. He gave me a thumbs up and said, "Don't worry, I got him!" That was all I needed to know.

I was on my hands and knees being careful not to raise up because two feet up above the gun barrel was a window through which he could see me if I raised my head. When I got within 30 inches of the gun barrel I could feel my heart pounding in my chest and throat. I took one deep breath and lunged over the barrel grabbing it with both hands and rolled forward snatching the gun from his grasp. My body flying through his door scared him so much he backed up into a corner of the hall and started crying while my partner and the sergeant ran in and cuffed him. I then had a desperate need to know if that gun was loaded. I found out it was when I jacked out three round of buckshot from the twelve gauge shotgun. That type of ammunition can do some serious damage. Believe it or not it was only then when I started shaking. I sat on the steps and thought to myself, "What the hell were you thinking?" The lawyer made me feel a little better when he approached me and said, "Gerald, I believe that's the bravest thing I have ever seen." "I'm glad you didn't have to kill him."

Later that same Christmas Eve night, I went to my parent's home where my wife and new son awaited my arrival. My sister and brother were also there with their spouses and kids. I picked up my son, held him tight, closed my eyes and thanked GOD I had made it through the shift. I didn't tell the wife what happened until the next day. I believe that was the best Christmas Eve ever. But this would not the last time I would have to deal with this gentleman.

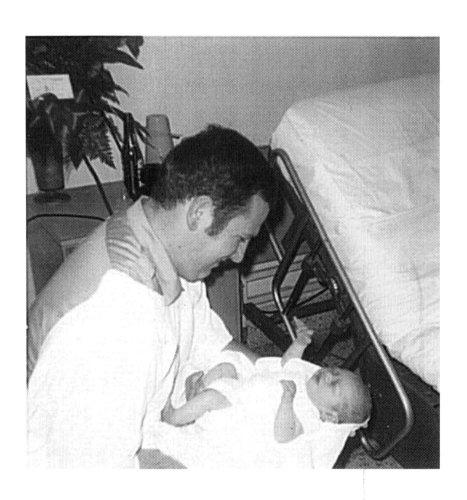

SOME PEOPLE JUST DON'T LEARN

Once again, I was working second shift on the North end of town when I heard a loud noise involving a vehicle that sounded like it had no muffler. I found the vehicle making the noise. It was a small sports car called a SAAB but it was loud and dragging its muffler causing sparks to come up as far as ten feet behind the car. I called the vehicle in using my walkie-talkie because my patrol car radio had been removed for repair. When I turned on my blue light the car sped up and continued to do so. I then turn on my siren and the SAAB increased speed to approximately seventy mph. The chase lasted seventeen miles and finally exceeded one hundred mph. A second patrol unit tried to pass the SAAB to get in front of him so we could sandwich him and slow him down. But as he tried to pass the sports car the SAAB snatched his vehicle to the left attempting to run the patrol unit off the road. My back-up then backed off. The chase ended when the vehicle came to a T intersection and he kept straight. By the way, did I mention it was a T intersection and there was no straight? I applied my brakes sliding to the edge of the road while the SAAB went air born landing between two very large pine trees and coming to rest on a bush that served to cushion his landing. The person driving the vehicle was the same guy from whom I had taken the shotgun in the previous story. Two times he was lucky but his luck wouldn't last much longer.

140 MPH, WHAT WAS I THINKING?

It was on a third shift night and there was a full moon. On a full moon night, you could cut your lights off and see just a good as if you had them on. Well, I was patrolling the West side of town (with my lights off) and had just pulled back onto the paved portion of the street. I pulled up behind a 1965 dark blue Chevelle but, because my lights were off, the driver never saw me. The driver sat at a stop sign and watched as my Sergeant drove pass in front of him. As the Sergeant turned into a motel parking lot to get a cup of coffee, the Chevelle driver floored his accelerator leaving black marks on the pavement 30 feet long and he was heading out of town. I was driving a 1972 Ford with a 429 police interceptor engine. His car was supped up and, as it turned out, was geared low for fast runs at short distances. My patrol vehicle was great on the top end but at that moment this guy was leaving me. My speed was climbing and I was six miles into this chase when I looked at my speedometer and realized I was approaching 140 mph. I remember thinking to myself, "What the hell are you thinking . . . it's just a speeding violation!" I took my foot off the accelerator to slow my speed and looked back up to realize I was going into a thick white cloud at ground level. In that cloud a tractor-trailer passed me heading in the opposite direction. I'm not going to say that scared me but my laundry man could tell you for sure. Anyway, I came out of the white smoke as quickly as I had entered it when I realized it was not a cloud. The Chevelle had just blown its engine. I was all into my brakes when I slid pass the Chevelle which was on the shoulder of the road. His engine was still so hot it was burning the grass underneath the vehicle. The Sergeant pulled up behind me about a minute or so later and we called out to the driver and his passenger to come out of the woods. They did. That turned out to be the fastest chase in my law enforcement career. And believe me I had plenty of them.

EVER HAD ONE OF THOSE DAYS?

I was working on second shift (had to be a full moon weekend) and it was on a Friday. I had just come off foot patrol downtown and was on my patrol vehicle when the vehicle in front of me stopped because the car in front of him stopped. Well, the car behind me rear-ended me, causing me to strike the car in front of me who, in turn, struck the car in front of him. We don't investigate our own accidents so the Highway Patrol had to come in and do it to avoid prejudice. Anyway, no damage done and the shift continued.

Less than an hour later I was on the same street heading the opposite way when I witnessed a vehicle pull out from a stop sign and into the path of a vehicle coming into down. The impact was so hard the vehicle (that didn't yield) overturned ending up on its roof.

About an hour after I finished that investigation I was driving by a convenience store when I saw a VW Beetle jump into gear and through the front of a convenience store. It was just one of those days when something happened it happened right in front of me. Those days are rare indeed! I'm glad it didn't happen often.

NEVER MESS WITH OLD TIMERS

It was on a full moon Saturday night when a call came in to police headquarters of shots fired on the East side of town at one of the clubs. The report was one person was down. Sound serious? Nope, it was funny as hell when we found out what had happened.

An older gentleman had gone to the club on this night to have a couple of beers, listen to the music and watch the younger folks dance. Well, that was his intentions until a young punk took exception to someone his age being there, walked over to him, pulled a hand gun and told the old gentleman to step outside. The old fellow never said a word. He just did like he was told and went outside. This was when the shooting started. Just like in the old westerns the young hoodlum told the old man to dance and firing his weapon into the area around the man's feet. The old man just stood there defiantly until he heard the wonderful sound he had been awaiting . . . the last shot and then click, click, click. Before the young fellow could reload his six shot revolver the old man took a few steps over to his pick-up truck, opened the door, reached in and pulled out a twelve gauge double barreled shotgun. The cocky young fellow saw this weapon of mass destruction and, without a bit of hesitation, took off running in an effort to distance himself from the old timer. However the distance he put between himself and the old man wasn't enough as the old guy leveled the shotgun at the fleeing man and fired both barrels. WOOOOM! WOOOOM! Both barrels found their mark striking the punk in the back right shoulder and the upper left thigh. The old man calmly awaited the police to arrive to explain what had happened. Numerous witnesses vouched for the nice old guy. We had to charge him by law but we also explained to the magistrate what the instigator had done. The magistrate released him on a written promise to appear without having to post a bond. It may have been a little different story if the man had anything other than bird shot in his shotgun. Anyway to continue the story, we located the young hoodlum lying between two houses a few blocks away but we couldn't approach him just yet. He had reloaded his weapon and was still firing rounds saying he would not be taken alive. We (officers) were lying on the ground behind a dirt ridge waiting for an opportunity to move in for the apprehension. That order never came because of our community service officers, who knew the suspect, talked him into giving up his weapon and giving up. Not waiting for Rescue to get there Monnie and I cuffed the suspect, placed him face down in the back seat of our patrol car and rushed him to the hospital . . . at twenty five mph. We didn't want to speed. How would it look for a Police vehicle to speed? Yes he was just fine and he learned a valuable lesson. Don't screw with old guys!

DRIVING UNDER THE INFLUENCE OF LOVE

It was a third shift night around 2:00 A.M. when I observed a vehicle driving in a residential area of town at a very slow speed. Believing I might be behind a drunk driver I followed the car for a few blocks. The car was weaving from the curb to the center of the road. I activated my blue light and the vehicle came to a stop. Walking up to the vehicle I quickly realized the driver wasn't under the influence when his date raised her head from his lap. I advised the driver to finish his exploits elsewhere other than the public highway and . . . to zip up his pants.

Did I mention that this guy was the same idiot who pulled a gun on the old timer in the previous story? The only difference was it didn't involve an old gentleman and he was using a different gun.

Same thing, different night!

It was another night on third shift when my partner, Monnie, called in he was stopping a cab on South Main Street, a possible D.U.I. I backed him up on the stop. When he was finished with the stop the cab drove off and he walked back to my vehicle with a big grin on his face. He told me the cab driver was driving all over the road so he stopped the cab believing the driver had to be under the influence. When he questioned the cab driver, the cabby used his thumb gesturing to the back seat where a young couple was having sex. The reason the cabby was all over the road was because he was trying to drive and watch at the same time.

For heaven's sake, get a room

Wouldn't you know the old sergeant was patrolling late one night near a residential area when he spotted a car parked in a wooded area on a dirt road. This road bordered an area known for criminal activity so he drove up behind the car with bright lights on carefully looking for anything suspicious. As he neared the vehicle he noticed both of the vehicle's back doors were open and a pair of feet hanging out of one side. He approached the vehicle on foot with flashlight and gun drawn. As he shined his light into the vehicle he observed a man who had apparently just hit overdrive while on top of his girlfriend. (Note: We refer to that as being "in the short rows.") The sergeant told the man he would have to stop what he was doing and move his vehicle somewhere else. The man, never slowing down, responded by pleading with the sergeant, "Give me a minute please, just one more minute!" The sergeant gave the man the extra minute and watched from his patrol car as the man finished, got out, put on his pants and left the area.

"I WOULD LIKE TO RESPECTFULLY REFUSE TO TESTIFY"

One night while patrolling the downtown area, I spotted four kids on the town's tennis courts and suspected they were consuming an alcoholic beverage of some type. As I drove toward them they saw me approaching and quickly ditched their (beer) cans behind a car parked a few yards away. Because all were under age I charged them with consuming alcohol in a public place being under age. Three of the boys were from rich families while one was an average Joe whose mother worked hard everyday to make ends meet. When court time came around I was called to the courthouse to testify. The judge was a very good and honest judge but very strict. He put up with no nonsense in his courtroom. When I arrived for the case I immediately noticed that only one of the defendants were at the defendant's table while the other three were sitting in the back of the courtroom smiling and giggling. The district attorney told me to take the stand to testify about the case. I asked him why only one was being tried in this case and not all four. He said the charges on the other three (rich) kids had been dismissed. I was fuming as I slowly walked to the stand and took my place in the witness box. The district attorney had me state my name and job title. He then asked me to tell the judge what happened. I sat there without saying a word. The D.A. requested again I tell the judge what happened. I looked at the Judge who asked me if there was a problem. I knew I was taking the chance of being charged with contempt of court but I looked at him straight in the eyes (trusting my judgment) and said, "Your Honor, I would like to respectfully refuse to testify in this case." He gave me "the look" and asked why. I told him that I had arrested four in this case and the District Attorney had dismissed charges on three kids who were from rich families. Now I was being asked to testify against the one who was not from a rich family. The Judge looked at me, leaned back in his chair and said, "Do you trust me to do the right thing?" I replied, "Yes your Honor, I do." He then said, "Well, trust me to do the right thing in this case and tell me what happened." Without hesitation I did just that. The judge, after hearing my testimony, sat back in his chair and gave the following judgment. "I find the defendant guilty as charged and sentence him to 30 days in the County Jail, suspended for 1 year on payment of court costs and $25 fine. Both the court costs and fine will be withheld and, at the end of the 1 year and if the defendant maintains a clean record, the charge will be removed from his record. The Judge then looked at me and said, "How did I do?" I replied, "Your Honor that was perfect and I thank you for it." I left the courtroom with a clear conscience and a stare from the district attorney. A few years later the young defendant told me how much he appreciated me going to bat for him and he would always remember that day.

TWELVE TICKED OFF LAWMEN

During court sessions, officers always sat in the jury box until their case was called. During one of these sessions a 19 year old man was brought before the judge for killing a dog. It wasn't that he killed a dog it was how he did it that bothered us so much. This low-life piece of humanity had been walking along the edge of a field when he saw a dog walking beside the road. He called to the friendly dog and the dog lowered his head, wagged his tail and walked over to the man. The man bent down and rubbed the dogs head as the dog wagged his tail enjoying the affection. While rubbing the dog's head the man reached behind his back, pulled out a large blade hunting knife and plunged it into the dog's chest and neck killing him instantly. When asked by the judge why he would do such a thing to an animal known to be a friendly pet, his answer was to shrug his shoulders and reply, "Because I wanted to." To make things worse the man showed no remorse for his actions. Every officer in the jury box that day wanted to give the man a little of what he had given the dog. Sometimes you meet people in life who deserve a painful end. This was one of those people. I still get mad today thinking about what he did to the poor unsuspecting animal and how he responded in court.

Quick response time

I was traveling to the police station one night to begin work on third shift. Approximately six blocks from the parking police parking lot I noticed a pair of bright lights approaching my car from behind at a high rate of speed. As the lights got closer I attempted to pull over to the curb to let this idiot pass by but it was too late. Before I could find the curb the vehicle had plowed into my left rear quarter panel. The car hit my full size station wagon so hard my police hat traveled from my head all the way to the back of my wagon. I was ticked! I grabbed my night stick out of habit and bailed out of my car with the idea of giving this idiot a piece of my mind. Then I saw the guy who struck my car. He had exercised his right not to wear a seat belt and his head had gone almost half way through his windshield and was a bloody mess. Here I was in my uniform with night stick in hand and I asked him if he was OK. His response was, "How the Hell did you get here so fast?" I responded with, "It was my car you hit!" His replied was, "Oh F**k!" He was taken into custody for Driving under the influence after his visit to the hospital.

Repeat Event on a Different Night

A year later the same circumstances were in place when I was heading to work for a third shift night. But this time I was turning into the police parking lot and the tail end of my unlucky station wagon had not quite cleared the street when a person pulled away from the curb looking behind them to make sure the way was clear and struck the right rear quarter panel of my car. This time it was just a matter of not yielding and not looking. No alcohol involved this time.

Drunk drivers do crazy things

Even in small towns people abuse their driving privilege by drinking before they get behind the wheel. There would be nights when I would apprehend three drunk drivers in a a three hour period and other times when I would only apprehend three in a month. Each person apprehended reacted differently to when stopped. That is, when they were able to have a reaction.

One of my nightly assignments was to watch the ABC store (also known as the liquor store) for the last 30 minutes they were open. Then I would follow them to the bank where they could make their nightly deposit. But every now and then something would happen to interfere with that task. One night a customer exited the store, got into his vehicle and proceeded to back into a town light pole. He then drove over the curb and onto a five lane street using all five lanes at a very slow speed. Using my blue light proved useless and finally using my siren brought him to a stop. I walked up to his window, knocked on it and told him three times to role down his window. He couldn't comprehend my instructions and was unresponsive so I opened his car door. When I did he literally fell out of the driver's seat and onto the pavement. When he hit the pavement his car started moving forward because he had left the gear shift lever in drive. After jumping into his vehicle to get it stopped, the man was arrested for D.U.I. He was transported to the station where he registered three times the legal limit on the breathalyzer.

Another night I was patrolling the North end of town and tried to stop a suspected drunk driver with my sergeant backing me up. The suspect slowed almost to a stop then jumped out and ran beside his car because he left it in gear. I knew if the suspect's car kept going there was going to be major damage to something so I had to make a quick decision. I ran down and jumped into his vehicle, got it stopped, jumped out and ran down the suspect (on foot) making a road tackle any NFL team would have been proud of. The whole time this thriller was playing out my sergeant sat and watched from about 50 yards away while having a good laugh on me. When I finally walked up to him (out of breath), he was still laughing but was able to give me a *"Nice tackle."*

A SCARY NIGHT ON THE EAST SIDE

It was on a full moon Saturday night when this officer was dispatched to the East side in response to a store owner who was having trouble with a man who wouldn't leave his store. On this particular night I had a new reserve officer with me and it was his second time out but the first time riding with me. We arrived at the store and there may have been ten people around just watching to see what was going on. Upon entering the store the owner pointed out the man who was refusing to leave. I spoke to the intoxicated man and convinced him to leave the property. But as we were leaving the store he decided he didn't like being escorted out so he stopped and called us MF's saying he wasn't going any M*****F***** where. Well so much for being nice. I placed him under arrest for disorderly conduct and when I took his right arm the reserve officer took his left. This man was big, stocky and muscular. As we were trying to cuff him the crowd had swollen to about eighty people and become very vocal trying to create an incident. Unable to budge his arm and noticing he was pushing back against me I looked down and spotted a blade in his right hand approximately three inches from my abdomen. I told the reserve, "He has a knife! When I tell you, back off and pull your weapon." He followed my instructions perfectly as we simultaneously backed off about ten feet and drew our revolvers. Due to the crowd size we had limited space to move around. They were shouting for the man to cut us. Being intoxicated his judgment was poor as he started walking in our direction with the blade still in his right hand. During this time I kept using my walkie to call for emergency back up. I was getting no response to repeated requests for help as the man drew nearer with the knife. I aimed dead center at the man's chest with full intent of taking a life if he came too close. Then the most beautiful sounds in the world reached our ears. It was the sounds of multiple sirens coming in for back-up support. I mean these cars were in the wind and when they turned the corners at each end of the block they were sideways with blue lights flashing and sirens and tires screaming. My department, the neighboring town's department, ABC department, sheriff's Department and the North Carolina Highway Patrol responded to my call for help. When an officer calls for help nothing else matters and that's when we find out just how much "We Are Brothers." But how did they hear my call for back up? I never got a radio response. As it turned out, during the struggle my radio had switched from channel 1 (the main repeater channel) to channel 2, a non-repeater channel. Only the dispatcher could hear me and she was upset because she knew my voice was in distress and she knew me as not being one to call for help. She started crying and calling everyone she could. Now let's finish this story because it just started getting interesting. My suspect threw his knife into the crowd so it would not be recovered and, as I said, the crowd was nowhere to be found when all the officers arrived. My suspect knew when the officers arrived he was in deep so he tried running. He ran down beside the store toward the darkness but forgot there was an eight foot fence surrounding the back of the store. He jumped up and started climbing the fence. Because I was so close on his heels, I was able to jump up, grab him and bring him down to the ground. About 30 minutes later after incarcerating my suspect I realized I had lost my eleven hundred dollar portable radio. Headquarters later realized that someone in the crowd found it because all night long someone kept keying it just to annoy us. But this story is not yet over because it just so happened one of our reserve officers was a full time post office employee who routinely delivered mail to the East side. The residents all knew him and he knew them so here is what happened next. He took a spare welfare (empty) envelope on his deliveries a day or so later around the time when welfare checks come out. He went to the area where the incident took place, held it up and set it on fire with his lighter. He did this in front of a crowd he new would be around the store. While the envelope was burning he told everyone if the police radio didn't show up soon more of these checks would burn or accidentally becoming lost. That same night, someone put the radio in the front yard of an officer who lived in the area. Who says the post office doesn't do good work.

Don't tell me Gut Feelings don't work

One night on third shift I was working the North end of town checking business doors and vending machines. The town had been having break-in after break-in for months with no clue as to the person or people responsible. The only thing we knew was the amount of damage caused during the break-ins far outweighed the amount of money stolen once entry was gained.

One of my vending locations was a church which had four vending machines sitting outside against the North wall of the church. I would check those machines at least twice each night when working the area. It was a late October night just before 2:00 A.M. when I took my second drive through the church property to check the machines. I did so with bright lights on because behind the church was a dense patch of woods. Behinds those woods about 100 yards was an apartment complex called Riverview Court. Once I made my second pass by the vending machines I turned onto the main highway and headed back toward my next location. I came to a stop sign about a quarter mile from the church and was about to make a left turn and head to my next stop when, for reasons unknown, something told me to go back and check the machines again. I didn't get these feelings often but they had always served me well and I remember being told by older officers to trust my instincts. This night I did just that. I turned my patrol vehicle around, got my speed up and coasted to church parking lot with my engine and lights off. When I made the hard left turn into the parking lot where the vending machines were located I turned on my high beams and there in front of me were two young men up to their armpits inside the vending machines. They took off when my lights hit them and into the woods they ran in full stride disappearing into the darkness. I called for back-up and started my foot pursuit into the woods maintaining communication with my buddy, Monnie by portable radio. I would stop every few seconds and listen to hear which way they were running. The noise they were making on dry leaves told me they were making a run toward Riverview Court apartments. I knew Monnie had his car in the wind so I told him which way they were heading and to watch them from the apartments. A couple of minutes later they walked out of the woods and into the arms of my partner. Man did I feel good when Monnie transmitted the following message; "Gerald, come on over, I've 'em both." As usual that's not the end of the story. We separated them at police headquarters and started interrogating them about previous break-ins. Each one was convinced the other had spilled his guts and by the time they both finished their confessions, fourteen break-ins had been solved and two more bad guys were off the street. This was a case when I trusted my gut and it worked for me.

The Continued Attraction of Vending Machines

Inside our recreation center there is a nice little bricked in area which holds a few vending machines. Each night before leaving the employees pull an iron gate shut and lock it in the event someone breaks in. Once the gate is closed there are only a few inches of clearance between the machines and the gate. One Saturday evening just before closing time an enterprising young man decided to hide until everyone had left the building. He then came out from hiding with his pry tool and climbed the gate guarding the vending machines. At the top of the gate he was able to lean over and pry open a Pepsi machine. This is where it gets good. The would-be thief was able to open the drink machine just enough to ease his way down (head first) into the space where the coin box was located. As his hand made contact with the coin box he lost his balance and fell head first into the machine where was lodged until Monday morning when the center opened for business. He was immediately found and the police were called. After spending two nights hanging upside down inside of a vending machine the thief was glad to be released from the machine. How he must have felt when the Sergeant looked at him and asked, "Want a Pepsi?" Because he didn't have any feeling in his legs he was transported to the hospital where he recovered quickly.

NEVER DRINK WHEN COMMITTING A CRIME

In my state of residence, we don't have neighborhood liquor stores like many other states. We have ABC (Alcohol Beverage Control) stores which are operated by the state. Just as in the preceding story we have another highly intelligent individual who decided to wait until the liquor store closed to climb up onto the rooftop of the ABC building. He then broke through a roof sky-light and lowered a rope down into the store. The rope had knots tied in it so he could more easily climb back out after he had stolen as much liquor as he could carry. There was only one hitch with this plan. He started celebrating too early before he started his first climb up and out. That's right . . . he got drunk as a skunk. So intoxicated in fact he was physically unable to climb the rope. As in the proceeding story, when the store manager opened for business the next morning he saw the would-be thief passed out on the floor surrounded by liquor bottles. The police were called and well, you know the rest of the story.

Dress for Success before you break in

I was working third shift one morning around 1:45 AM on the North end of town when the officer on the South in called for back-up. He was on foot checking doors when he heard glass break and observed a man running from one of our banks. From the limited description of the suspect and direction of escape given on the radio I radioed the sergeant telling him I would be setting up on a street that separated the business are from the East side. I felt sure the suspect would be crossing this particular street at some point. Again my gut paid off when I saw a lone male walking briskly across the open stretch of road. As soon as I started my vehicle the man took off running and the chase was on. I kept the man in sight until he cut across a residential yard. I stopped my patrol car and bailed out only 50 feet or so behind him when he disappeared through some vines and weeds. When I tried to follow him I bounced off a high chain link fence which was covered with the vines. The suspect apparently knew where the hole was in the fence which told me he lived close by. The sergeant called in a request to the local prison to bring in their dogs known for their tracking abilities. When the dogs arrived they immediately picked up the suspect's trail and tracked the scent right to the front door of a home one block over from where I had lost sight of him. The sergeant knocked on the door several times until a little old lady responded and opened it. He asked her if there was anyone in the house with her, to which she replied, "Just my grandson." The sergeant found the young fellow and immediately noticed he was sweating profusely after he questioned him as to his whereabouts over the last hour. Of course he had been in bed and had not left the house all night. The sergeant then asked him to get dressed and come down to police headquarters for further questioning. The suspect slipped on some brown pants and a shirt then we all went to the station. After several denials the sergeant asked me if I could identify the man I was chasing. I answered honestly saying, "No Sir, I never saw his face." I told the sergeant the only thing I knew without a doubt was the man I was chasing had on bright green pants. He asked me if I was sure because these brown pants were the ones he put on when he got out of bed. I said "Yes, I'm sure!" The sergeant and I went back to the residence where he asked the grandmother if he could look around the house. She was very cooperative and allowed the search. The sergeant looked around the young man's bedroom finding nothing. He then walked a path from the bedroom to the front door and there, behind the woman's living room couch on the floor, was a pair of bright green pants and they were still wet with sweat. He came to the door and held them up with a smile. He said, "Are these the pants you saw?" "They sure are!" I replied with a sigh of relief.

It was great to have a sergeant who didn't doubt his officers. This was surely a confidence builder for me.

DON'T BE THANKFUL FOR A QUIET NIGHT UNTIL IT'S OVER

It was December 21st at 5:26 A.M. and we had just finished making our last rounds for third shift tour. We had gathered on the police station steps and decided it was time for a coffee break before conducting our daily morning house check. We had not been out of the station parking lot more than two minutes when the dispatcher called to all cars saying he thought someone had just shot into the police station. We all responded with lights and sirens to find someone had indeed opened up with a shotgun using buckshot firing through the glass entranceway of the station. It didn't take long to figure out who fired the shots from a nearby alleyway. A seventeen year old had just been released from jail a short time before the incident after having been charged and jailed earlier in the evening and was angry at the police. He had gone to a friend's house where he obtained the shotgun so he could get even with the police. When arrested for this charge he was held in jail until his trial. After spending a lot of time picking up buckshot from the police lobby floor we realized how lucky our dispatcher was that the customer window did not face the door. And we three were lucky because we had departed two minutes before the shots were fired.

The shotgun blast came from the fenced area to the far left.

CALL IT WHAT IT IS, A HOMICIDE

I had worked first shift on the day this happened and was not part of the investigation. But I don't mind telling you the results of this investigation left a bad taste in my mouth.

A well known elderly businessman in our area (80+ years old) used to go walking every afternoon in and around the area of his residence. He was known to carry a fair amount of cash on his person at all times just like he was known to always come home within an hour after his walks. This particular afternoon he began his walk and was last seen in the town common when a strong storm arrived very quickly. The detective later said he believed the senior citizen became disoriented in the storm and walked into an area where he was unfamiliar. His body was found the following morning underneath a railroad trestle about 8 blocks from his home. The detective insisted the incident was an accident with the man not being able to see the train tracks or the openings between the railroad ties under the trestle. My partner and I felt it was a robbery and murder due to the following things found at the scene. First there was no money found on the victim and we knew he had money. Secondly the victim's shoes were placed neatly beside the body when found as if someone had picked them up with one hand and sat them down beside him. The third and final thing which bugged us was when my partner and I went to the railroad trestle and found drag marks on the wooden railroad ties. This would explain why he was without shoes. We shared this information with the detective but he had made up his mind it was an accidental death and didn't want to change his mind.

I had attended high school with the victim's grandson and tried to contact him several times over the years with no success. I did finally get a chance to share the information with him one evening when we finally met at my wife's school class reunion. He was appreciative of the information. More importantly, my conscience was clear.

SOMETIMES THERE IS NO JUSTICE

It was on a Sunday morning when the sergeant radioed me to meet him at the station. When I arrived we rode together over to an address on the East side of town. We knew something was up when we drove up to the house and there was a small group of people on the opposite corner. Although they were staring at the house no one would say anything so we went to the front porch and knocked on the door. We then spotted a blood trail leading into the home. After knocking on the door again and receiving no reply we pushed open the door and called to any occupants. Still receiving no reply we followed the blood trail through a door into a small foyer with doors on the left and right. The blood trail took us to the left. Straight inside the door there was a bed to the left which held a small boy of about 6 years of age and he was still asleep. On the right in the same room across from the boy's bed was a couch on which a female laid naked from the waist down. She had a deep gash across the entire width of her forehead and was obviously deceased but our main concern at the moment was the child. We pulled the patrol car closer to the home and, in a smooth motion, tossed a blanket over the child blocking his view of his dead mother and quickly removed him to the patrol vehicle. Once there a female friend of the family sat in our vehicle with the young fellow. In his sleepy state he really didn't know what was happening but accepting of the lady who was holding him.

The sergeant told me to look around outside the premises for any evidence while he notified rescue and the coroner. I followed the blood trail to a 2 x 4 piece of board which turned out to be the murder weapon. This was on the back porch. I then walked into a small patch of woods behind the house and found the murderer passed out on the ground and still intoxicated from the night before. Before finding out the woman, his girlfriend, was deceased he admitted striking the woman with the board. So we had our victim, we had our murderer and a child now without a mother. When our man went to trial his admission meant absolutely nothing. The autopsy showed she died from the blow on the head which was obvious to us. But his lawyer asked for a second autopsy and the request was granted by the court. The second autopsy showed the victim died from (are you ready for this) acute alcoholism. The murderer walked free due to conflicting autopsy results. There was no justice in this case.

Dead Bodies Ruin Your Day

If anyone stays in law enforcement long enough there are going to be DB (dead body) calls. The worst kind of DB call is one when you walk up to a door and you can already smell death. This took place when my fellow officers went to the East side of town to check on a store owner who had not been seen nor had his store been opened his store for over two weeks during the hottest part of the summer. He lived beside the store so the officers didn't have to search very long. When they approached the door of his home they knew he or something was dead inside due to the odor. The door was dead-bolt locked so a window had to be broken to gain entry. Opening the door from the inside officers searched the house and found the decaying body of the owner in bed where he had obviously died in his sleep. But to complicate matters the rats had found him prior to the police and had eaten the tips of his fingers, toes, earlobes and nose. He lived by himself and had no living relatives therefore the store was never reopened.

In another DB case, there was a lady in our town who had on and off issues with depression and would, on occasion, take an overdose of assorted pills to end her life. She would feel the pills start to take affect, have a change of heart and call the police to report what she had done then ask for the rescue squad. The police and the rescue squad always got there in the nick of time and all would be well with the world until about three or four months later when she would repeat the process. This happened numerous times over the years until one night she called us, we responded and dispatched the rescue squad only to find out she had waited too long to call us this time. She finally got her wish and left this world. This was a nice lady too.
(Note: If you hear I have committed suicide, it's a lie.)

My sergeant and I responded to a call one morning when an employee from a local florist failed to show up for work. We arrived at the employee's home where his employer was waiting on the porch. He opened the front door and we walked in to find the employee's body in the bedroom lying back on his bed. He had been deceased for some time and there were no signs of foul play. A quick look around the bedroom provided us with enough information to know the young man had taken his own life. His right shoe and sock was off and at the end of his bed was a .22 rifle. He had used the rifle to place against his chest and, using his big toe, pulled the trigger. As far as suicides go this was the neatest one I had ever seen. A small hole in his shirt and only a couple of drops of blood stained the shirt where the bullet had entered the body. At approximately 30 years old he had ended his young life for reasons unknown before he had a chance to live it. We awaited the rescue squad and coroner because that's all we could do at that point. The time waiting had me wondering why someone so young would do this. What in his life would have been so bad that he would want to end it? Now we will never know.

No ma'am, you're not dying on my shift

The sergeant and I were riding together on third shift one night when we drove by our town commons. The sergeant stopped for a stop sign and was about to proceed through the intersection when I spotted a young female sitting on the curb on my side of the patrol car. I told the Sergeant to stop and back up. We stopped, backed up and spoke to her a couple of minutes. Her demeanor and speech indicated being intoxicated or being on drugs. We both knew at this time of night (early morning) it was not safe for a female to be all alone in that area. The sergeant told me to place her under arrest so we could take her to the jail. That way we knew she would be safe until she at least sobered up. I decided not to cuff her so I placed her in the back seat and sat on her right side with a hold on her right wrist. As the sergeant was driving slowly to the jail I loosened my grip on her wrist but quickly found that my hand felt like it was almost adhered to her wrist. I told the sergeant to cut on his interior light which he did. I then told him to turn around and get to the hospital. He asked why and I told him that the girl had cut both of her wrists. He slammed on brakes, turned around, took a look and he put that 440 magnum engine in the wind. We got her there in plenty of time and the young girl recovered. I'm thinking it was meant to be that I spotted her small figure sitting on the curb that night. She had been sitting on the curb waiting to die. We didn't let that happen.

Playing Tricks on Fellow Officers Helped Brighten Spirits

First of all, this trick is still done today. At shift change we would get out of the patrol vehicle, remove the key, turn on the blue light, siren, windshield wipers, radio and anything else that functions when the key is turned on. Then when the next officer gets into the vehicle, inserts the key and starts the vehicle, everything would activate at once and send the officer into panic mode and make many references to your mother! That was always fun . . . still is.

THE BEST TRICK EVER ON A FELLOW OFFICER

This has to be one of the best tricks of which I have ever been a part. In the early morning hours one third shift night my working partner, Monnie and I were together on one vehicle. The dispatcher was an officer who normally would be on the street but tonight he was working the desk due to a testicular issue. He was a good friend to both of us but he would not be on the street until his "issues" returned to normal. Well, Monnie rode past the dispatcher's house where his wife was sleeping and shinned the light on his license plate, wrote it down and started smiling. I didn't know what he had in mind but I knew it was going to be good. We rode to the edge of town where no one lived close by. Monnie cut on his siren and called in a 10-80 (a chase) shouting he was in pursuit of a vehicle traveling at a high rate of speed and gave the direction. He then called in the license plate number of the vehicle being chased . . . the dispatcher's license plate number. There was a few seconds hesitation before the dispatcher came back on the air and shouted, "Stay on him Monnie, stay on him, that's my car, I repeat, that's my car!" Monnie then cut the siren off and slowly pulled out onto the highway heading back toward the station. When we walked into the Police Station door the dispatcher looked at us with his basset hound eyes and said, "You sons-of-bitches know how much trouble you just got me in?" We were laughing so hard we were crying when the dispatcher continued, "I just called my wife and gave her hell for leaving the keys in the car." "She told me the car was still in the carport." "You got me . . . I have to admit . . . you got me!"

Being a breathalyzer operator

In my third year on the department, I was selected to attend breathalyzer school because of the needs of our department and our shift. During the three day class we took one day of classroom study followed by one day of operating the breathalyzer and one day of drinking. Yes, I said drinking. The second day saw us dividing the class into half with one side drinking and the other side consuming alcohol. Then the next day the roles were switched. Now to tell you the truth I'm not much of a liquor drinker and if I do partake, I like the smooth stuff. Because this class was given by the state they bought the cheapest, nastiest, worst tasting thing they could buy. I still remember the name of it today . . . OLD DOVER! The way it tasted, it should have been named old rover. They tried to make it better by telling us we could use as much chaser as we needed so I brought two 7-Ups. It didn't help. They assigned a certain number of ounces to be consumed by certain individuals and wouldn't you know they picked me to consume the most. I hated it but I got it down long enough to take the breathalyzer test. I blew a .11 on the model 900A Breathalyzer. Then I got up, went to the men's room and heaved up everything I had consumed. When my wife showed up to transport me home (as per our instructions) I threw my books in the front seat, climbed into the back seat and laid down. I remember I told my wife, "Don't say a word, just drive!" I got my breathalyzer's license and over the next two years ran tests for every law enforcement agency in our town and county.

ONE BREATHALYZER TEST THAT SCARED ME

One night, while working second shift, my partner Monnie had arrested a woman after she backed into a gas pump at one of our local gas stations. He brought her in for a breathalyzer test. I could see she might weigh a hundred pounds and stood maybe five feet tall. Now before I finish this story the highest reading I had ever obtained in a breathalyzer test was in the low twenties and to be considered under the influence the suspect had to register at least a ten or .10, but this night would be different. I took the breath sample and waited the necessary time period. I then flipped the toggle switch which indicates whether a person has been drinking. The alcohol indicator needle took off like a scalded dog to the left side of the screen and pinned itself to the left side. This indicated there was definitely alcohol in the suspects system. Now I had to find out how much. I now have to turn a balance wheel until the needle hits dead center. When her reading reach .30 I was questioning myself as to whether I had done anything wrong. I looked at Monnie and he could see my concern. He, being an operator also, said "You've done everything right, just keep turning the wheel." I did and soon the needle started to move. To keep this story moving she wound up with a breathalyzer reading of .38. According to guidelines I had to run a follow up test to make sure her reading wasn't going up. If the reading increased we had to take her to the hospital due to a potential for her to go into a coma. But she didn't and her second reading was at a .36. We just took her to jail.

A COLLEGE EDUCATION MAY BE OVERRATED!

Once every six months all officers were required to qualify with their assigned firearms. This experience was supervised by the old, experienced, been around for ever sergeant. You know the one who has the least patience with young rookie officers? The one who doesn't like to repeat himself and always has something negative to say about everything? Yes you know someone like that. Well on this wonderful event filled day there were two incidents worth mentioning. The second incident involved shooting clay pigeons with riot guns. One officer who lacked a great deal of coordination was the third one to try his luck at this. The first two officers had done fairly well. Keep in mind the round clay disks were hand launched from a metal platform on the ground by pulling a spring and rope mechanism. Who pulled the string you ask . . . you guessed it . . . the old sergeant. He had pulled two times already and the third officer hadn't even come close to striking the clay pigeons. On the third pull the anxious officer was so gung ho to hit the clay pigeon he fired his shotgun into the ground three feet in front of the squatting sergeant as soon as the launching rope was pulled. After the sergeant brushed the dirt off of his shirt and pants he got up, walked over to the officer removed the shotgun from his hands, handed it to another officer and said, "Somebody else do this sh**, I'm done!"

But the best part of his day came when we qualified with our revolvers. Here's how it happens. We have ten metal frames with each one holding one piece of cardboard. On the cardboard we would staple a paper silhouette of a human and inside the silhouette were numbered zones. We would have to shoot left handed, right handed, standing, kneeling and lying on the ground. After firing 50 rounds with our weapons, we would yell "clear" and approached the silhouettes to score them. We would then gather in the middle of the range and report our scores to you guessed it, the sergeant. Then we would staple another paper silhouette to the cardboard backing and do it all over again.

During one of those reporting sessions, a young reserve officer and an N.C. State graduate with an degree in engineering spoke up saying, "sergeant can I make a suggestion to you which might help you speed the process up a little bit?" The sergeant replied, "Sure if it will help speed things up!" Are you ready for this? The college grad reserve officer said, "Why don't you staple ten silhouettes to the cardboard then, after firing the 50 rounds, just peel the front silhouette off?" We all stopped, turned, looked at each other while trying not to laugh and anxiously awaiting the sergeant's reply which we knew would be priceless. And it was. He replied, "I'll tell you one damned thing, if my wife says one word about sending our son to college, I'm going to punch her right in the mouth!" It took us quite a while compose ourselves and longer for the State grad to get the embarrassment off his face. We never let him live that down.

Ever been hit by the President of the United States?

I believe it was my fifth year as an officer when our department was chosen as one of several departments to participate in the protection of President Carter when he visited Wilson, NC, a neighboring town 40 miles away. Because of the small size of our department only a few of us could take part in this major event. Before we could participate however the Secret Service and the FBI had to conduct background checks on all officers to make sure we had crime free histories. Once done, we were good to go.

The President was to stop at the city library where he would make a speech. He then would leave that location and go to a local tobacco warehouse to help inspect and grade local tobacco product. He would then leave. Sound simple? No, not really. Before we received our assignments we had to meet with the Secret Service in the basement of the library where we were given some specifics. For instance, we were told about lapel pins. There were people wearing certain pins that would allow them to come within twenty five feet of the President. Other pins would allow people to come within ten feet of the President. Then there was THE lapel pin which would allow people to walk up and hug him if they wanted to. We were also given specific instructions on how to handle the press, especially those who would not listen to instructions. The last thing they told us was, "No one, and I mean no one, was to drive down the road beside this library!"

After our instructions were received we left the library. This is when we found out our department would be the ones assigned to the street where the motorcade would park upon arrival. In the street at the area where the motorcade was to park was me. I was very anxious about what was about to happen and I was determined no one was going to enter my area of responsibility. Just a few minutes before the motorcade arrived, a full size black

Chevy containing four men in dark suits and dark glasses turned onto our street but the officers at that end never stopped it. When it reached my area I stopped it and asked for identification. The man without question showed me his Secret Service credentials. I apologized to him and reminded him we were told no one was supposed to be on the street. He looked at me, smiled and said, "You were exactly right to stop me and verify who we were." They drove away but others had taken their place. As a helicopter started circling overhead, I saw people on rooftops, on either side of the sidewalk which led to the library steps and the most impressive to me, a guy who was about 50 yards from me inside of a fully extended bucket truck wearing a black suit, dark sunglasses and holding a rifle with a scope. Oh yeah, no nerves here. Then the motorcade pulls up. I held my position in the middle of the street. The first car was the secret service people who bailed out while it was still moving. The second car was the President's car which came to a stop beside me. The trailing cars included the Governor, senators and congressmen. The secret service formed a half moon shape around the President's car facing the crowd and the press who had gathered directly across from me to get a good camera shot. Then, unbeknown to me, the President's car door would not open so he could step out on the sidewalk as planned, so he had to get out on the street side. Who was standing there and received a bump by the Presidents door? Yours truly! He smiled that Jimmy Carter smile and said "Sorry about that." I replied, "No problem, Mr. President." He then walked around the back of the limo and toward the crowd on the library grounds. There was this one photographer who kept trying to get closer until I warned him he would be arrested if he came any closer. He backed off when warned. As the President walked up the sidewalk, another man tried to hand the President a home grown watermelon. As he presented the watermelon a Secret Service person ran up grabbed it and ran across the front lawn of the library. They took no chances with his safety.

Well, the President made his speech, returned to his car and left for some tobacco warehouses. Our job was done and everything went off without a hitch. The secret service was happy and we were tired.

Always keep one eye on the Sergeant

Sometimes the sergeant on duty would make sure we were physically shaking doors at night so he would set little traps. An example would be to place clear tape at the top or bottom of a screen door to see if we pulled it open to check the main door behind it. If you didn't he would chew the officer's s butt. Another trick would to be take dark thread and string it across an alleyway to make sure you patrolled through the alley at night. Imagine one officer not trusting another. It always bothered us that while he would ride around watching to see if we were doing our job, his areas of responsibility would experience the break-ins. Remarkably no one ever said anything out loud about the double standard.

How do old Sergeants stay safe so long?

Being a rookie cop was difficult only because I always wanted to do things the right way and I certainly didn't want to embarrass my fellow officers by overreacting or under reacting in a situation. I have always known why God gave me two ears and one mouth so I always listened twice as much as I spoke. The old sergeants taught me another valuable lesson about surviving a long time in police work.

One night I was working the North end of town when we received a call of a fight taking place on the East side. I radioed to the sergeant asking him if he wanted me to meet him at the scene. In a very calm and unconcerned voice, he replied, "Nah, just meet me at the station," which I did. I jumped out of my car and into his just knowing we would be literally flying over to the East side to break up the fight. Nope! He backed up slowly and pulled out into the street going less than the speed limit. My mind raced wondering why we weren't getting there right now to stop the fight and keep someone from getting hurt. Finally, I came up with enough nerve to ask the Sergeant why we were going so slow when we could be breaking up a fight. His reply not only made sense but it allowed me to see through his eyes. He said, "Why race over there and get into the middle of a fight and possibly get ourselves hurt or killed when we can take our time, get there as the fight is ending and arrest who's left standing. These proved to be words to live by.

Threatening an Officer's Family is NOT a Good Idea!

One night on third shift night I received a call about a vehicle striking a telephone pole on a deserted stretch of road near our elementary school. When I arrived, the driver was still behind the wheel and very intoxicated. He complained about being hurt so, as required, I transported him to the emergency room to have him checked. For whatever unknown reason he started becoming belligerent toward me threatening to kick my ass which didn't bother me. What did bother me was when his anger increased and said, "That's all right you son-of-a-bitch . . . I know where your wife and baby live!" I can honestly tell you this. I became so angry so quickly I could see nothing but red in both eyes and I believe I hit him. I didn't see it and I didn't feel it until it was over when my normal sight returned and my hand hurt. His mouth was bleeding and he was cursing me more than before. The emergency room doctor stepped behind the curtain and said "What's going on here?" I told him the man had just threatened to get my wife and baby and I believe I may have hit him. The doctor looked at me, then him and said, "Well, let's take a look." The Doctor checked the man turned around and said, "Well, as far as I'm concerned, he hit his mouth on the steering wheel." I said "Thanks, doc" and he replied, "No problem!"

I wish I could tell you this was the end of the story but the man just wouldn't let it go. When I was nicely escorting him out of the E.R. he continued to curse me and kept repeating what he was going to do to me if I removed the handcuffs. Finally I had had enough. I spun him around and took my cuff keys out and started to remove his cuffs. He said, "What are you doing?" I said, "I'm going to take these cuffs off so you can whip my ass!" He suddenly changed his tune and kept turning to keep my cuff keys away from him so I could not remove his cuffs. Then the apologies started and continued until he was jailed. But, again, that's not the end of the story.

On court day the defendant pleaded not guilty and took the stand to tell his side about the accident. He then told the judge I had struck him. The judge, knowing me as a person of calm demeanor, looked at me and asked, "Officer Ward, did you strike this gentleman?" Without hesitation, I answered, "I believe I did Your Honor." "And why did you hit him, officer?" I answered, "Because he threatened to harm my wife and baby your Honor." The Judge looked at the defendant and asked, "Do you have any more questions for this officer?" He replied he did not. The Judge without hesitation said, "Guilty!"

Writer's note: My actions on that night were wrong and completely out of character. This was the first and only time I would lay hands on another person in anger. I think we both learned a lesson that night.

Putting Life in Perspective

It was a second shift early afternoon when our department received a request to go to the hospital to assist an officer from our neighboring town with an unruly person he had arrested. The officer needed back up because he wasn't physically able to handle the hostile individual in his custody. Two weeks before this, the officer had undergone through exploratory surgery in his abdominal region due to constant pain. The doctors closed him up telling him there was nothing they could do for him. He had terminal cancer with only a short time to live. The officer then pulled up his shirt and showed me a long line of stitches which started at his breastbone and went down to his navel from the recent exploratory surgery. When I arrived at the hospital emergency room he was relieved to see me because there was no more fight left in him. The suspect had already resisted so much the officer had to use his black-jack on him and opened up a gash requiring numerous stitches. He couldn't spend much time with me because he had to stay near the doctor while he sewed up the intoxicated individual.

As he walked away, I heard a man's voice entering the hospital and the voice sounded desperate. I couldn't leave my fellow other officer but I could see the other man entering was covered with blood and he was carrying a child that appeared to be around five or six years old. The little boy he was carrying was completely limp. I'll never forget his pleas as he walked into the E.R repeatedly saying, "Someone help me!" I later found out he had been mowing his lawn on his riding lawn mower and didn't know his little son was running behind him. He put the mower in reverse and backed over the child. The child had already expired when he arrived at the hospital. I always remembered the man's look of desperation. When I bought my first riding lawn mower I made sure if my son came outside he would always be in my lap. That way I would always know where he was.

A Great Doctor

There was a woman in town the county the sheriff's deputies would have to arrest on a regular basis. On this particular night the woman was so intoxicated and mean, she attacked a deputy sheriff. She was so aggressive the deputy had to hit her with his "black-jack." This action injured the woman which required the deputy had to transport her to the hospital for stitches. While there she was cuffed to the E.R. bed but there was nothing to be done about all the vulgarity coming from her never resting mouth. It was MF this and MF that with other colorful language mixed in. The doctor had been called away from his supper table and was not in the best of moods upon his arrival to deal with the female drunk. After a few minutes of enjoying the language being spewed by this individual, the doctor prepared a syringe to numb the area he would be stitching. He quickly became so tired of the never ending filthy words he started injecting the numbing solution into the scalp then quirt some into her mouth. He repeated this process until the intoxicated woman was incoherent with her profanity. All was right with the world. Did I mention he was a great doctor and loved the officers?

Not much sympathy for hardheaded people

I was trying to sneak in my thirty minute lunch one day on first shift. While sitting at the table trying to wolf down my food a person came up to me and stuck a card in my face. The card had a keychain attached to it and the writing on the card indicated the person was a deaf-mute trying to make a living for his family, etc. etc. etc. You know the routine. Well, our town has a city ordinance which states you can't go person to person or door to door unless you are a church or you obtain a license to sell inside the city limits. I wrote this down on a sheet of paper and gave it to him. It also said that if he continued I would be forced to place him under arrest for illegal solicitation. He nodded his head OK and walked out the front door. When he left, he made a sharp left turn which put him heading toward the grocery store next door. I followed him from a distance and observed him walk up to a customer in the store and hand them the card. I wrote on my pad, "You are under arrest!" and put it in front of his face. I took him to the magistrate's office where he plead guilty and paid the fine and court costs with cash . . . a big roll of cash! I then watched him go to his brand new full size Cadillac and drive away.

Lady, You Weren't Speeding . . . You Were Flying Low

It was on a Sunday morning and the sergeant instructed me to work radar on a five lane highway which held a 35 mph speed limit. It was around 10:30 on a Sunday morning, the traffic was light and all was quiet until my radar started going haywire. At first, I thought the radar might be reacting to power lines overhead because the speed was showing way over thirty five and nothing was in sight. Then I recalibrated the unit and it activated. I looked up to see a light green Chevrolet topping the hill leading to my location and this car was floating due to high speed. I fired up my patrol vehicle and as the car passed my location at seventy two mph. I turned on the blue light and pulled the vehicle over. Inside the car was one of the most beautiful young ladies I had ever seen, but I had a job to do. I took her license and registration back to my vehicle where I started writing the citation. The next thing I knew this young lady put her head inside my vehicle window with her face about six inches from mine and said, "Officer, can't you let me go this one time?" I told her I could not due to her high speed. Then she said "I will do anything, anything you want me to do if you let me go this time!" I was somewhere I wasn't supposed to be and my parents can't find out." I swallowed hard and firmly replied, "Ma'am, you need to go back to your vehicle and wait for me to finish writing this citation, then you can be on your way!" She did just that. I wrote the ticket and gave her a copy. Did I mention she was gorgeous? I'm talking cold shower gorgeous.

Writer's note: This was one of those citations which never made it to court. The charge was dismissed without my knowledge or my permission. (Politics strikes again).

Every town has a Charlie Boy . . .

You know, every small town has a character with their own unique way of saying and doing things. Their exploits in a small town rapidly spread all over the community. One of our characters was a person we knew as "Charlie Boy." He was one of those people you could count on to ask you what you were doing while you trying to do it. Rumor has it he was walking around town one day and came across a town employee who was digging a hole. Charlie Boy stopped and watched him a few minutes then approached the worker asking, "Hey, What you doing?" The worker answered, "Digging a hole, Charlie Boy." Charlie Boy asked, "What you going to put in it?" The worker answered, "Charlie Boy, we're going to put every S.O.B in town in this hole." Charlie Boy stood there a few seconds then responded, "Well, who will be left to cover up the hole?" Yes, you too have a Charlie Boy somewhere in your town. Beware of them . . . they vote.

THEN THERE WAS BUDDY

Another memorable character we sometimes dealt with was a man we called "Buddy." He was built like a fire hydrant and as strong as an ox. He would sometimes act like he was crazy and at other times he seemed to be just as normal as everyone else. The first time I met Buddy was when I was in training and walking the beat downtown. My training officer looked at me and said "Watch this." He looked at Buddy and held out a dollar saying "Buddy, walk on your hands for me." Buddy would immediately throw his legs straight over his head and walk on his hands until he was told to stop. He always got his dollar too. But the thing I remember about Buddy the most was what he would do each December a day or two before Christmas. He would always do something crazy to get himself arrested and taken to the magistrates office where he would request to be sent to Goldsboro (know for its mental facility). His request was always granted by the magistrate. Everyone knew why he wanted to go each December around the same time. He told us the mental hospital had the best Christmas parties of any place he had ever been then he would be released to return home the day after Christmas. Say what you want, he was one smart crazy person.

Don't Tick Off My Partner!

One night at the beginning of third shift, my partner came to me and said he had received word one of our illustrious town councilmen had made the statement that if any officer ever arrested him for drunk driving or anything else, he would see to it the officer was fired. My partner looked at me and said, "You know what this means don't you?" I said, "I sure do, we're going to catch him!" My partner replied, "You damned right we are!" We knew it probably wouldn't be hard to do as the married Councilman was known to frequent the local bars and pick up younger women. We tried and tried to catch this guy but he would never show himself around town late at night late at night. We later heard that he was aware of we were looking for him. He made no further statements.

Monnie Got Me This Time

One day while working 1ˢᵗ shift, Monnie asked me if I had ever been to a pig killing. I looked straight at him and told him I had not but always wanted to see one. He gave me directions to his Uncle's home where the pig killing was to take place. Now before you start getting upset pig killings have been going on since time began normally taking place in the fall of the year when the weather is cool and flies are no issue. Farm people (before supermarkets) use to hunt, kill or grow their own food. Some down here in the South still do it the old way. Plus it's quick and painless to the pig. Now, let's get back to the story.

Monnie had told me before arriving at the farm, all I had to do was wait until the owner pointed out the pig. Then I was to jump the fence and chase down the animal until I caught it. I would then have to turn the pig around facing the farmer who would use a .22 rifle to shoot the pig in the forehead. Well hell, I was excited being at my first pig killing and was more than ready. Several of us walked up to the fence and the farmer, holding his .22 rifle, pointed out the one he wanted. Over the fence I went and had run about fifteen steps when I heard everyone laughing. I knew Monnie had pulled one on me yet again. I should have known better. He yelled to me to get back on his side of the fence before I got shot. Then the farmer went to work doing what he does best. The farmer leveled his rifle and made a noise he normally uses when he feeds the pigs. When he did this every pig stopped in their tracks and turned around and stared at the farmer. Pop went the rifled and down went a pig. The farmer then ran up to the pig and shoved a knife in the neck and down into the heart to let the pig bleed out. This rids the pig of the blood so when the pig is cleaned or dressed out, there is no mess to deal with. After the pig was prepped it was slow cooked and basted on the grill (pig cooker) until ready and, later that day, fed several families.

Big Monkey

Another example of Monnie's sense of humor was a night when he and the acting sergeant were patrolling on the West side of town when they spotted a extremely intoxicated man who didn't seem to be making much progress trying to walk. They knew the man and decided to give him a ride home instead of the county jail. But Monnie had a better idea. He just happened to have with him a gorilla mask. He put the mask on and got into the back seat while the acting sergeant spoke to the intoxicated individual offering him a ride home. The subject agreed to the ride, like he had a choice. The acting sergeant opened the back door to the squad car and helped the man into the seat. On the way home, the acting sergeant kept speaking to the man and glancing into the rear view mirror to see if he had noticed the gorilla sitting beside him. The man finally made a slow turn to his right and saw a 6' 3" 280 lb gorilla sitting beside him looking back at him. Monnie grunted and the man quickly looked forward. Arriving home the man slowly turned and looked again. The gorilla was still staring at him and grunted again. The passenger's eyes were as big as saucers but he never said a word. Monnie was cracking up underneath the gorilla mask as the acting sergeant, crying by now with laughter, got out and opened the back door of the patrol car helping the man out. As the man started to walk past the acting sergeant, he stopped, looked at him and quietly said, "Did you know there's a monkey in the back seat?" The sergeant replied, "A what?" The guy responded, "A monkey . . . a big damned monkey . . . in the back seat." By this time Monnie had slipped out of the car and ducked down behind the car so the intoxicated individual could not see him. So when the intoxicated man told the Sergeant about the monkey in the back seat he tried to show the sergeant but . . . there was no monkey. As he made his attempts to get into his house, he kept looking back at the car. I'm pretty sure he was wondering if he had seen what he thought he had seen.

My working partner, like me, could see his police career going nowhere and for the same reasons. Neither of us was willing to kiss up to get ahead nor did we play politics. We felt politics should never interfere with officers doing their job nor should we have to worry about who we arrested or to whom we issued citations. So after years of working together and making one hell of a team my buddy decided to change professions. He found a good job as a railroad detective and moved away his life long home. But let me tell you how I got him before he left. You'll love this.

The Big squeeze

Monnie were riding together on a Sunday afternoon just before we were to separate and go to our respective ends of town. He decided he had to go pee so he drove down a small dirt road which ran below the railroad trestle. This leads a small turn around spot beside the river where people would sometimes go to fish. It was deserted when we arrived and he got out of the car to relieve himself. I exited the passenger side. He walked over to the river's edge, looked around and pulled out his personality and started to urinate. We were about 15 feet apart when I heard his water hitting the river water. I slowly removed my revolver from my holster, pointed it at the ground beside me and discharged one round. Damn that was loud. Then I heard Monnie groaning in agony as his water had cut off completely and he started calling me every S.O.B. in the book and telling me I was now responsible for his penis now being shaped like an hour glass. Then came the lame threats of retaliation in the last week before he left the department. I was ever vigilant awaiting his pay-back which never came. He left the department a week later and quickly established a great reputation at his new job. It was no surprise to me. I knew Monnie would do a great job wherever he went. It didn't take us long to miss the big guy.

Losing a Best Friend

One of the saddest nights of my life was when I found out my ex-working partner, Monnie, had lost his battle with heart disease. His nephew called asking me if I would be a poll bearer at Monnie's funeral. When I told him I would be honored he started crying as did I. To be chosen to carry the man who always had my back and was the best police officer I had ever known was truly an honor. I couldn't believe he was gone. My emotions were really screwed up on the day of his funeral. With tears rolling down my face, I kept trying to think of something else to keep myself under control. But all I could think of was my big buddy, a police buddy, a tough cop who backed down from no one and an all around great guy who would have taken a bullet for me. He was a hell of a man standing around 6' 3" and around 280 lbs. It was still hard to believe this big fellow was gone until I saw him at our home town funeral home. He needed a heart transplant but knew deep down it would not be forthcoming. Knowing his days were numbered he took care of everything ahead of time so his wife would not have that burden. Like I said, he was a hell of a man and met death just like he met life . . . head on.

After placing his coffin on his final resting place and laying a rose on the top of the casket I walked away and cried uncontrollably as memories flashed through my mind as well as the close calls we both had. He earned the respect of everyone with whom he worked and I believe they all came for his funeral. I have never met another man like Monnie nor have I ever seen a funeral like the one he had that day. I know we will patrol together again when my life's tour of duty is done.

Time to Try Something Else

After spending approximately ten years wearing a uniform, I could see I had gone as far as I would be allowed to go considering the leadership I had to deal with every day. The same person who "advised" me to turn in the award I have received for Officer of the Year found out I had applied for a job with the highway patrol. I was asked if I wanted my captain notified of my application. I told the officer definitely not and told him why. My first day back on the job after my days off found me observing the same HP representative talking to my captain. I had a bad feeling about that and the bad feeling proved true the following day. When I arrived for work the captain called me into his office. He quickly turned on the arrogance and superior demeanor, looked at me and said, "I understand you have applied with the highway patrol." Being honest, I answered, "Yes Sir, I have." He didn't beat around the bush as he responded the following way; "Well, I'll tell you there's a lot of people out there who would love to take your position with this department so you have a decision to make before you walk out of my office. You can either withdraw your application to the highway patrol or you can turn in your badge." "Now what is it going to be?" Because I had a wife, a small child and one on the way I never hesitated when I replied, "Captain, I will notify them today that I will not be going forward with my application."

That man built a fire in me that helped me decide I would never be held under anyone's thumb again. From that day forward, I was looking for something better. I would eventually take my talents to the private sector even if I had to start at the entry level . . . and I did just that.

Good things come to those who wait.

I was working radar one morning in a thirty five mph zone when the rescue squad passed my location in excess of eighty mph. I did not pursue the vehicle but I did tell the sergeant about the speed. He told the captain who went to the rescue squad and told them if they ever exceeded the posted speed by more than fifteen mph again the driver would receive a citation.

Wouldn't you know it, a few years later the Captain had an attack of kidney stones and called . . . the rescue squad. They picked him up and he asked them to get him to the hospital as quickly as possible because of the pain. But as per the captain's instructions they drove no more than fifteen mph over the posted speed limit. What goes around . . .

A Highway Patrol Story

Now I will tell right up front, I don't know this to be true or not true but I think you will like it. A Highway Patrolman told me one day that he was working radar in a particular area of the state outside of my county. He was working a fifty five mph zone when a man came through doing sixty eight. He pulled out an expected short pursuit but when he put on his blue light, the man sped up to over eighty mph. The officer then put on his siren and pulled beside the speeder and motioned for him to pull over. The speeder looked at the patrolman and pulled over. The officer, ticked off because of the man's actions, walked up to the speeder's window and obtained license and registration. The officer then looked at the man and said, "Mister, you give me one damned good reason why you sped up when I put my blue light on you and I might cut you a little slack." The man looked straight into the patrolman's eyes and said, "Officer I am so sorry for doing that but six months ago my wife left me for a highway patrolman and I thought it may have been you trying to giver her back!" The patrolman handed the man's license and registration back and said, "Sir, you have a nice evening" and walked away.

True or not, I don't know. I just wanted to share the story.

A Stand-in Mother Duck

The following story is not one I experienced but one told to me by a close friend. Glen and his wife often went to a campground which had lakes on the property. One day while walking the edge of one of the lakes Glen found about a dozen or so duck eggs along with the mother duck which had the appearance of having just been stoned to death. Glen, being the soft hearted nice guy he is, gathered up the eggs, brought them home and put them in his incubator. As I recall his story all but one egg hatched and guess who Momma was? Yep! Glen constantly spoke to his ducklings and they followed him everywhere. He even bought a plastic swimming pool and built a ramp so his dirty dozen could easily walk up to the pool and jump in for a swim. He even had them trained with a box so when he called them they would all come to and enter the box. Here is where it gets good. One day Glen decided to take his box of ducklings to a field a block away and allow them to walk and feed in the two feet tall grass. Once the ducks left the box they could not been seen due to their small size.

So picture this. Here is a lone man standing in a field turning around and talking to himself while holding a box. Someone apparently saw this unusual activity, became nervous and called the police. The officer arrived, stepped out of his car and slowly approached Glen, not knowing he lived close by. He asked Glen what he was doing and Glen responded, "Walking my ducks." The officer looked around, looked back at Glen asking him to repeat himself. Glen told him a second time he was walking his ducks. The officer, according to Glen, got this strange look on his face and said something into his shoulder microphone. He believed the officer might be calling for back-up so he started calling his ducks. They all arrived around the same time and climbed into the box in front of the officer who, by the way, suddenly had a look of relief on his face. Glen then told him the story about the ducks and walked back to his yard a block away. Glen said it was one of the funniest moments he had ever had with the police.

As for the ducks, Glen had a friend who lived out in the county who had land on which a large pond rested and was found to be perfect for ducks. He had raised the ducks with the permission of the state's wildlife officer and he had fulfilled his "motherly" duties. He released his duck family at the new home he had found for them knowing they would soon be on their way to places unknown just as God intended. Glen was and is truly one of God's earthly angels.

Change is good

Ten years and three children later I still loved law enforcement and have a great respect for the badge. But I couldn't see myself overcoming the always present departmental politics. Knowing I would never be able to advance in a small town I left for greener pastures. But that is another story spanning twenty five years. I think I feel another book coming on . . .

Our three children, the youngest of which is now 32.

Keep in mind every department, no matter the size or location, has it own moments of excitement, sadness, levity and craziness. It happens every day while we are in the comfort and relative safety of our homes. Remember the people in uniform representing the thin blue line are all that protects us and our loved ones from evil people who have never and will never respect the law or law-abiding people. They are out there and they will always be out there. The good news is . . . so are the good guys.

MEMORIES OF A SMALL TOWN COP

Thanks also to all the men and women who wear a badge. You are the people no one wants to see unless you are needed. You are the people without whom all citizens would be in danger. You who are the fine line separating good from evil, the ones who receive no kudos for a job well done and the chosen ones who are sometimes overlooked for a pay raise during budget crunch time.

May the people who wear the badge always be there when needed, show compassion when summoned, make the correct decisions when called upon, protect the helpless in their time of need and stay safe while doing all the above. And may you always go home safe at the end of your assigned shift.

Do your job well and use this one simple rule to guide you; Remember it is better to be tried by 12 than carried by six.

There's nothing like kids coming to greet Dad for lunch.